Winning the Chores Wars

HOW TO GET YOUR CHILD TO DO HOUSEHOLD JOBS

Lee Canter and Marlene Canter

Effective Parenting Books

Contributing Writers
Patricia Sarka
Marcia Shank

Book Design
Joyce Vario

Cover Art and Design
Richard Rossiter

Editorial Staff
Marlene Canter
Carol Provisor
Barbara Schadlow
Kathy Winberry

© 1996 Lee Canter & Associates
P.O. Box 2113, Santa Monica, CA 90407-2113
800-262-4347   310-395-3221

Printed in the United States of America
First printing April 1996
00 99 98 97 96   10 9 8 7 6 5 4 3 2 1

ISBN #0-939007-74-6

Household Jobs

A PART OF EVERY FAMILY'S LIFE

I can't do the dishes. I have to do my homework now. I'll do them later.

That's not my job. Sarah is supposed to do it.

Why do I have to do everything? It's not fair.

Do these statements sound familiar? If so, read on.

Everyday household jobs like feeding the dog, doing dishes, taking out the trash and picking up dirty clothes often lead to everyday arguments between parent and child. Sometimes it seems easier just to do the job yourself! You may wonder if all the hassle is worth it.

Relax. Children should be expected to take part in household responsibilities. In fact, keeping a household running smoothly is the responsibility of every family member—kids as well as adults.

Here's why:

- Today's busy families cannot run smoothly without everyone pitching in and doing their part.
- Taking responsibility for household jobs helps a child develop into a responsible, self-reliant adult.
- Learning how to start and complete a household job develops self-confidence and self-esteem.
- Working together with other family members on household jobs builds cooperation and encourages teamwork.
- Doing household jobs with parents and/or siblings can be a fun-filled, sharing experience.

Household jobs are an opportunity for your child to shine. When you give your child responsibility for a job you are saying, "I have confidence in you. I believe in your ability. I know you can do it!"

The Job Squad

A PROJECT FOR THE FAMILY TEAM

Your family is a team—at work and at play. When it's time to do household jobs let your family work team, the Job Squad, get the job done.

Who can join the Job Squad?

Every family member from toddler to old-timer can and should help around the house. It's important for your child to see that your family is a team working together, and that he or she is an important, contributing member of that team. Your child may complain about jobs, but in truth your child's self-esteem will soar when given responsibility.

> "This is a family, and we all cooperate to keep this family together. I have my jobs to do inside and outside the home. You have your jobs, too. School is one of your jobs. Household responsibilities are another. As a family, we're a team. And you're an important part of our team. We need you!"

The three Job Squad lists that follow will give you an idea of what jobs are appropriate for your child.

Junior Job Squaders
Ages 3–5

Toddlers and preschoolers really do enjoy helping around the house. Take advantage of their enthusiasm! Encourage your Junior Job Squaders with household jobs that are done as a team with a parent and older siblings. Demonstrate one job at a time and remember to be a patient teacher. Make a game of household duties by singing songs or sharing stories while you work.

Suggested jobs:

- pick up toys
- make bed
- help parent set/clean off the table
- help parent rinse the dishes
- help parent wash the car
- help parent sort the laundry
- help parent shop/put away groceries
- help parent prepare meals
- help parent dust
- help parent rake leaves/water lawn/plant
- help parent care for family pet
- help parent with younger brother or sister

School-age Job Squaders
Ages 6–9

Although homework is a top priority for school-age kids, there is still more than enough time before and after school and on weekends to help around the house. School-age Job Squaders can be assigned jobs that require more responsibility. (Suggestion: Keeping one's room clean should be a child's responsibility from age 6 up.)

Suggested jobs:

- clean up own room
- pick up toys
- make bed
- put dirty clothes in the hamper
- set or clean off the table/rinse dishes
- dust/sweep
- empty the garbage
- clean the sink
- take care of the family pet
- prepare simple meals for self (sandwich, salad)
- prepare sack lunch for school
- help parent wash the car
- help parent sort or fold the laundry
- help parent shop/put away groceries
- help family with yard work
- help with younger brother or sister

Adolescent or Teen Job Squaders
Ages 10–13
Older children tend to procrastinate when it comes to household jobs. Keep your older child organized and on a schedule. Household jobs should be done before TV or play.

Suggested jobs:
- clean up own room
- make bed
- put dirty clothes in the hamper
- set or clean off the table
- wash the dishes or load the dishwasher
- dry the dishes or unload the dishwasher
- dust furniture
- empty the garbage
- mop floors/vacuum rugs
- clean sinks, tubs, windows, mirrors
- take care of the family pet
- prepare simple meals for self
- prepare sack lunch for school
- help prepare family meals
- wash the car
- load the washing machine/unload the dryer
- help parent shop/put away groceries
- help with yard work
- help with younger brother or sister

The Job Squad Program

Most children just need a little help getting organized and staying on track with household jobs. The Job Squad program will help your child do just that.

The Job Squad program is broken down into four steps:

Step 1: Getting Organized

Step 2: Assigning Household Jobs

Step 3: Teaching Your Child How to Do a Job

Step 4: Encouraging Your Child

If you follow the simple steps of the program, most of the problems you have getting children to do household jobs will disappear.

It's not 100% foolproof, though. Some children may still balk at household duties. If parents have been consistent and fair—and problems still exist—then they must take further action. The Job Squad program includes a plan of action to help solve this problem, too.

The Job Squad Program

GETTING ORGANIZED

The first step in the Job Squad program is to decide what jobs need to be done around your home—and who can do them.

Use the Job Squad Planning Sheets on pages 57–58 to help you figure out:

1. all the jobs that need to be done around the house,

   and

2. who can do those jobs.

Job Squad Planning Sheet

Household Job _____ ___

Household Job _____ ___

Household Job _____ ___

Household Job _____ ___

Household Job _____ ___

Household Job _____ ___

Household Job _____ ___

Household Job _____ ___

Household Job _____ ___

Household Job _____ ___

Household Job _____ ___

Household Job _____ ___

Write down all the household jobs that need to be done.
Write down the initials of family members who can do each job.

Need help deciding what jobs your child should be responsible for?

Refer to the job lists on pages 8–10 for specific jobs that are appropriate to your child's age group and work your specific jobs in accordingly.

First, on the Job Squad Planning Sheet make a list of all the household jobs that must be done every day or every week to keep your house running smoothly. Be sure to include some of your own responsibilities so your child can see that you are a working member of the Job Squad, too!

Next, decide which jobs your child is able to do. Write his or her initials next to those jobs. Add your own initials to jobs that are earmarked for you or other adults. (If you have more than one child in the Job Squad, be sure to fill out the sheet for all children.)

The Job Squad Program

ASSIGNING HOUSEHOLD JOBS

In Step 1, you made a list of all the household jobs that need to be done on a daily or weekly basis. You also noted which jobs your child (or children) is capable of doing.

Decide who will do what.

Now's the time to decide which Job Squad member will do which household job.

You have three choices when handing out jobs:

1. You can decide what jobs your child will do.
2. Your child can decide what to do.
3. Combination of both 1 and 2.

Keep in mind that there are some jobs you may need your school-age child to do (make his or her own lunch, walk the dog, empty the garbage), especially if you work outside the home and your time is limited. That's OK. Explain to your child that just as you have certain jobs you must do, it's equally important that he or she does these specific jobs also.

Involve your child in the job selection.

Your program will be most successful, however, if your child feels a part of the decision-making process on some jobs. Here are three ideas to make this process more fun.

"Help Wanted" Ads

Each week post a list of household jobs that your child is capable of doing and let him or her make several choices.

In the examples that follow, notice that each ad describes exactly what the job will involve. Use the "Help Wanted" signs on pages 59–60 to create your ads.

HELP WANTED

Table Setter—*Must be able to set table neatly with placemats, dishes, knives, forks, spoons and napkins for breakfast and dinner.*

HELP WANTED

Pet Keeper—*Makes sure the dog has dry food and fresh water in the morning and gets ¹/₂ can of dog food and more fresh water before 6 P.M. every night. Occasional dog biscuits, too.*

> ## HELP WANTED
> **Dust Buster**—*Using clean cloth and furniture polish, dusts all tables and chairs in the family room, dining room and living room every Saturday.*

> ## HELP WANTED
> **Trash Trasher**—*Empties kitchen garbage into outside garbage can every evening after dinner. Empties all other trash cans into outside garbage can on the day before garbage pickup.*

I Pick, You Pick, We Pick

Here's a job-choosing activity that is great to use if you have more than one child. This method gives both you and your children some decision-making power. You will need a stack of 3" x 5" index cards for this activity. Here's what to do.

First, write the name of each household job you need to be done during the week on separate index cards. On each card write the names of your children who are able to do the job.

Next, lay the cards out on a table. Tell one child that first you will pick a job you want him or her to be responsible for in the upcoming week.

> *"Mark, this week I'd like you to set the table each night. I know you can do a good job at this."*

Then, tell your child to pick a job he or she wants to do.

"I'll feed the dog this week."

Finally, pick one out together.

"How about folding the laundry? Would that be OK with you?"

Repeat the process with each child until the cards are gone or until you decide that your children have an appropriate number of jobs. After one or two weeks, repeat the process, allowing your children to take on new responsibilities.

Spin-a-Job

This game of chance is fun for one child or the entire family. Cut out the spinner (directions are on page 61) and attach to the center of the Spin-A-Job wheel. Then have your child spin the spinner several times. Whichever household jobs the spinner lands on become your child's jobs for the week.

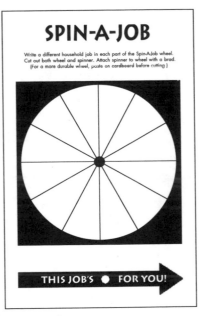

SPIN-A-JOB

Write a different household job in each part of the Spin-A-Job wheel. Cut out both wheel and spinner. Attach spinner to wheel with a brad. (For a more durable wheel, paste on cardboard before cutting.)

THIS JOB'S ● FOR YOU!

Record the final assignments.

Once jobs are assigned, circle the appropriate initials on your Job Squad Planning Sheet to show who is doing what job. Post the sheet on the refrigerator to remind all family members of their responsibilities.

STEP

3

The Job Squad Program

TEACHING YOUR CHILD
HOW TO DO A JOB

Once you know which jobs your child is expected to do, you need to make sure he or she knows how to do them. Remember, one of your goals is for your child to experience success in carrying out a responsibility. Your child can't be successful unless it is clearly understood how you expect a job to be done.

Decide how you want the job to be done.

Here's what to do:

Using 3" x 5" cards, write down the steps involved in doing a specific job.

For example:

Job: Feeding the dog.

Step 1: Get the dog's bowl.

Step 2: Wash and dry the bowl.

Step 3: Open can of dog food and put in bowl.

Step 4: Put empty can in trash, and spoon in dishwasher or sink.

Step 5: Put bowl on porch.

Step 6: Refill dog's water bowl with fresh water.

Teach the job to your child.

After you've completed the card, demonstrate the job for your child—step-by-step. Then have your child repeat each step after you.

- Be patient.
- Be supportive.
- Review the steps often.

Give your child the checklist as a reminder of the steps involved in doing a good job.

Make sure that your child clearly understands how to do each job he or she is responsible for. Make sure that you've gone over the steps with your older children as well. Often, we wrongly assume our older children already know how to do a job.

Make the goal participation, not perfection!

Your child's beginning attempts at household jobs may not be perfect. That's OK. Through trial and error and lots of repetition, your child will eventually become better at setting the table, making her bed, feeding the cat, or matching his socks. The most important outcome is that your child will feel the pride of being a useful, contributing member of the family.

Start slowly. Don't give your child more new responsibilities than can be handled. Give your child a chance to succeed at one responsibility before adding another.

4

The Job Squad Program

ENCOURAGING YOUR CHILD

The best way to encourage your child to continue doing a good job is to give plenty of praise when a job is well done. Children love hearing how much you appreciate their Job Squad efforts. Paired with a big hug and kiss, praise can make your child feel proud—and loved!

Use "super praise" to motivate your child.

Here's an idea that two parents, or a parent and another adult, can use to make a child feel appreciated and noticed.

First, one parent praises the child:

> *"You did a terrific job cleaning up your room today. I want to make sure Mom hears about this when she gets home."*

Next, this parent praises the child in front of the other parent:

> *"Sarah's room looks great. She really worked hard cleaning it up."*

Finally, the other parent praises the child:

> *"I'm so proud of you, Sarah. Dad told me that you put a lot of effort into your room. You're doing such a great job!"*

If you're a single parent, you can use a grandparent, a neighbor, or a family friend as your partner in giving "super praise." Any adult whose approval your children will value can fill the role of the second person offering praise.

Give your child plenty of praise for effort as well as accomplishment. Don't expect perfection, but do expect cooperation.

A Job Well Done

10 WAYS TO SHOW YOUR APPRECIATION

♥ **Job Squad Celebration**

When your family team is cooperating and getting the household jobs done as expected, fill out a "Super Job Squad Award" on page 71 for each child. Treat your family to an outing (movie, picnic, museum)—after all, this is a significant accomplishment!

♥ **A "Pat on the Back"**

Trace your handprint on a colored sheet of paper. On the front write, "Jessica deserves a pat on the back for helping around the house." On the reverse side, write something special you will give your child for a job well done. (For example, "For doing the dishes every night, Jessica is awarded lunch or dinner at her favorite restaurant—and no dishes!")

♥ Hidden Treasure

Hide little treasures where your child will find them while doing household jobs. A thank-you note (or P.S. I Love You Coupon, pages 69–70) placed in the clean laundry pile pinned to one of your child's t-shirts is a fun discovery. As your child puts away clean clothes, he will find the note that says, "I just wanted to say thanks for putting away your clothes."

♥ Extra! Extra! Read all about It!

Watch your child's eyes light up when she sees her name in print. Place a thank-you message in your local newspaper or throwaway advertising magazine (i.e., Pennysaver). Many newspapers will print these messages free of charge.

♥ The Sounds of Music

While your child is doing household jobs, play his favorite CD or cassette. The job will go faster when accompanied by a familiar tune.

♥ "Crafty" Thank You's

Going shopping? Stock up on craft materials (clay,

paints, yarn, noodles for mosaics). In recognition for continued good work, give your child an afternoon of craftmaking—clay sculpting, straw painting, yarn weaving or noodle mosaics.

♥ A Refreshing Break

Surprise your child with a refreshing, homemade fruit popsicle after finishing his or her household jobs. Frozen cranberry, orange, or apple juice makes a "cool" snack treat.

♥ A Penny Saved...

Reward your child with a penny each time she completes a household job. Have your child place the penny in an empty jelly jar. At the end of the week, have your child count the pennies and record this amount in a special "bank book." When your child saves ten pennies, for example, treat her to a movie or special event.

♥ Household Job Swap Ticket

JOB SWAP TICKET

The Job Swap Ticket (pages 67–68), allows your child to swap a household job for a day. Award this ticket to your child for doing a thorough job (with no complaints or reminders) with household chores. He can give this ticket to any family member and swap a household job. (For example, your child might swap taking out the trash for setting the dinner table—especially when he has something special to do after dinner.)

♥ **Wonderful Week**

Reward your child's effort at the end of a week of doing household jobs by giving a "Wonderful Week Job Squad Award" (page 72). This is not an award for perfection; it is simply another way to say, "Thanks, I know you're trying, and I appreciate it!"

Job Squad Daily Planner

FOR GETTING ON TRACK

Your Job Squad program will be most successful once your child gets into a comfortable routine of doing household jobs. The best way to do this is by careful planning and follow-through. Your child may need some help developing a Job Squad routine, so we've included two helpful tracking sheets.

First, does your child need reminders about when jobs are to be done? If so, use the Job Squad Daily Planner!

Job Squad Daily Planner

Wednesday		
Morning	Afternoon	Evening

Job Squad Daily Planner

For _____

Fill in your morning, afternoon and evening jobs for each day of the week.

Sunday		
Morning	Afternoon	Evening

Monday		
Morning	Afternoon	Evening

Tuesday		
Morning	Afternoon	Evening

Here's how:

- The planner (pages 62–63) divides each day of the week into morning, afternoon and evening segments.

- Decide which jobs should be done on which days during each segment.

- Write the jobs in the spaces provided.

- Hang the planner up and your child will have an ongoing reminder of what needs to be done and when.

- Encourage your child to check the planner in the morning, after school and at night.

Job Squad Tracker

FOR STAYING ON TRACK

The Job Squad Tracker (pages 64–65) lets your child track jobs and work toward a specific goal. Here's how to use it:

- Meet with your child to decide which jobs he or she will be responsible for during the upcoming week.

- Write these jobs on the chart. Place the chart in a convenient place—refrigerator, bulletin board, kitchen cabinet door.

- Have your child mark an X on the chart each day a job is completed.

- Check the chart each day. If your child has forgotten to do a job, give a gentle reminder that his or her goal may be in jeopardy if the job isn't completed.

- When your child reaches the goal (for example, all jobs completed for five days), reward the accomplishment with a special treat or a P.S. I Love You coupon (pages 69–70).

Planning will help make it happen and within a few weeks your child may no longer need these written reminders.

Household Jobs Problems

SUGGESTIONS AND SOLUTIONS

Should you have problems getting your child to do household jobs, don't despair. By following these problem-solving steps you will quickly pinpoint the specific problem and discover quick and easy solutions that will get your child back on track.

First, pinpoint the problem.
As you read the problems listed below, check the one(s) that apply to your child.

☐ **Problem A:**
My child doesn't complete household jobs on time.

☐ **Problem B:**
My child needs to be reminded to do household jobs.

☐ **Problem C:**
My child complains about doing household jobs.

☐ **Problem D:**
My child dawdles while doing household jobs.

☐ **Problem E:**
My child doesn't complete household jobs according to my standards.

Then, take action.

Take a look at the suggestions presented for each problem. Try the solution(s) that you feel will work with your child.

PROBLEM A:

My child doesn't complete household jobs on time.

A. Give your child verbal reminders or leave notes. (Tape a note to the bedroom door that reads, for example: "Please clean your room today by 6:00.")

B. Teach your child how to make a personal time schedule that includes household jobs.

For example:

Bryan's Day	
3:15–3:30	rake leaves
3:30–4:30	play with friends
4:30–5:30	do homework
5:30	set table
After dinner	feed dog, take out trash

C. Give your child plenty of praise each time a job is completed on time. That more than anything else you do will encourage your child to continue the responsible habits.

PROBLEM B:

My child needs to be reminded to do household jobs.

A. Keep your child "posted" with Post-It™ notes. Place friendly reminders on the bedroom door, bathroom mirror, or refrigerator. "Don't forget, it's leaf-raking day!"

B. Purchase an inexpensive bulletin board or chalkboard. Get your child into the habit of checking the board every day for important messages and household job reminders.

C. Complete the Daily Planner on pages 62–63, post it in a conspicuous place, and encourage your child to check it daily.

D. Place a copy of the Job Squad Tracker (pages 64–65) on the refrigerator door and on your child's bedroom door. Highlight the chores with a fluorescent marking pen. Give your child stickers to paste on the chart when a job is completed.

E. Reward your child's positive behavior with the P.S. I Love You Coupons on pages 69–70.

F. Purchase a "kid calendar" or an inexpensive appointment book to help your child schedule household jobs.

PROBLEM C:

My child complains about doing household jobs.

A. Ask yourself, "Have I been fair in handing out household jobs?" Maybe your child has a legitimate complaint. Review everyone's household responsibilities and discuss them with your child. Make sure that siblings are treated fairly, and that the less desirable jobs are rotated.

B. Ask yourself, "Have I explained how important it is that everyone in the family helps out?" Get the teamwork message across and complaints may stop.

C. Ask yourself, "Do I always tell my child how much I appreciate the help?" It's easy to forget, but your child may just need to know that his or her contributions are appreciated.

D. Have your child put any complaints in writing. Then discuss them and really listen to what your child has to say.

E. Start a No More Complaints Counter. Make a chart with five squares. Each day that your child doesn't complain, put a sticker in one square. When all five squares are filled, rent a special video or make a special dessert for your child.

PROBLEM D:

My child dawdles while doing household jobs.

A. Play "Beat the Clock." Use a kitchen timer to keep your child on track. Set the clock to the number of minutes you expect the job to take (for example: unloading the dishwasher may take 10 minutes).

B. Motivate with music! Challenge your child to finish a household job before the end of a favorite song. (Longer jobs may require a few songs or an entire tape or CD.)

C. Your child may need a goal to work towards. If the job is finished in a timely manner, reward your child with a P.S. I Love You Coupon on pages 69–70.

PROBLEM E:

My child doesn't complete household jobs according to my standards.

A. First ask yourself, "Have I taught my child exactly how I expect the job to be done?" If the answer is no, review pages 19–21.

B. Ask yourself, "Am I asking too much of a child at this age?" Make very sure that your expectations do not exceed your child's abilities.

C. Ask yourself, "Am I giving lots of praise for my child's efforts?" It is very important to reward your child's efforts with kind words and a big hug.

D. Reteach the job. Sometimes children just forget, or they need to be reminded how to do the job correctly. Repetition will probably solve this problem.

A variety of "take action" ideas have been offered for each problem. If you find that one suggestion is not effective with your child, try another. Keep in mind that you are not just trying to get jobs done. You are also guiding your child toward responsible behavior that will help him or her grow into a self-reliant adult.

If, however, problems persist in spite of all you do, you will need to take further action.

If problems persist...

✔ You've explained why jobs are a shared responsibility in the family.

✔ You've taught your child how you expect his or her jobs to be done.

✔ You've given lots of hugs and praise when the jobs are done.

You've taken all these important steps, but your child still is having problems doing jobs responsibly and you don't know what to do.

...it's time to use the Job Squad Contract.

A Job Squad Contract is a written agreement between you and your child that states:

1. The household-job rule that must be followed.

2. The specific reward your child will receive for following the household rule.

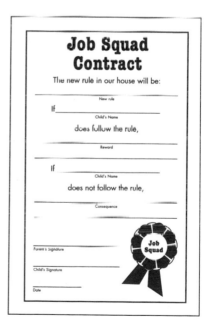

3. The privileges that will be taken away if your child doesn't do the assigned household jobs.

Follow these steps for establishing the rules, rewards and consequences you will use in the contract.

1. Establish the rules for doing household jobs.

Meet with your child to talk about the problem. Explain that you are instituting a new rule in the house. Depending on the problem your child is having with household jobs, the new rule may be:

- Do all assigned household jobs each day.
- Complete household jobs on time.
- Complete household jobs according to standards agreed upon.
- Complete household jobs without complaining.
- Do household jobs without being reminded.
- Other_____

Say to your child, for example:

> *"Brian, I want you to be more successful in doing your jobs on time, so I've come up with an idea that I think will help you. First of all, we're going to have a new rule at home. The new rule is this: All jobs will be completed on time."*

Write the new rule on the Job Squad Contract (page 66).

2. Establish the rewards for following the rules.

Decide how you will reward your child for following the rule. For example, your child may:

- Be awarded a P.S. I Love You Coupon.
- Be given a special award.

- "Rest" on the seventh day if all jobs were finished each day for six days.
- Stay up later on the weekend if all chores are completed Monday through Friday.
- Have a friend stay overnight.
- Watch a favorite video with Mom and Dad.
- Other _____

Say to your child, for example:

> *"I know you can follow this rule, and when you do I want to recognize your good work with something special. If all your jobs are completed on time Monday through Friday, you can stay up later on the weekend nights."*

Write the reward on the Job Squad Contract (page 66).

3. Establish the consequences if the rules are not followed.

Decide what loss of privilege would be effective in helping your child follow the new rule.

Explain to your child that if the rule is not followed, a privilege will be lost. Choose a privilege or activity that is meaningful to the child—one that will serve as a deterrent. Explain that losing this privilege is your child's choice—and it won't happen at all if the rule is followed.

Here are some ideas. (You, of course, know best what consequences would be most meaningful to your child.)

- Lose TV privileges.
- Lose phone privileges.
- Lose the privilege of playing outside with friends.
- Lose after-school sports participation privileges.
- Other_____

Say to your child, for example:

> *"Brian, if you don't choose to follow the rule,
> you'll lose a privilege. That means if jobs are
> not completed on time, you will lose TV privi-
> leges for that day."*

Write the consequence on the Job Squad Contract
(page 66).

Sign the contract and date it.

Once the contract is completed, sign and date it. Then
post it on a cupboard, bulletin board or the refrigerator door.

You must be consistent. If your child breaks the rule,
you must follow through with the consequence—each
and every time. Likewise, if your child follows the
rule, you must provide the reward. You are the key to
making the contract work. It will be effective only if
you follow through.

How to Speak

SO YOUR CHILD WILL LISTEN

Does your child tune you out, ignore you, or argue with you when you ask him or her to do household jobs (or anything else, for that matter)? If this is commonplace in your home it may have a lot to do with the way you are speaking to your child.

Parents who are successful in encouraging better behavior speak to their children in a clear, direct and firm manner that leaves no doubt about what is expected.

Parents who are ignored or argued with often speak in a way that is either wishy-washy or hostile.

Do any of these comments sound familiar?

"How many times do I have to remind you to take out the garbage?"

"Won't you please try and get your chores done today?"

"It's six o'clock and your room is still a mess."

"Why can't you put your dirty clothes in the hamper?"

Chances are you've said things like these many times. Most parents have. But what do statements like these really say to your child? Look at each one carefully and you will see that they either ask pointless questions, beg, or make an obvious statement of fact. In any case, they do not tell the child what you want done. They do not let the child know without a doubt that you expect the garbage to be taken out, the chores done on time, the room cleaned and the dirty clothes put in the hamper. Wishy-washy statements don't let your child know that your words are to be taken seriously—that you mean business.

They make it easy for your child to ignore you.

And what about comments like these?

"I should know better than to expect you to get your chores done on time."

"I've had it. If you forget to do the dishes one more time you're really going to get it."

"That's it. You're grounded for two weeks."

What do these all-too-common remarks say to a child? Put-downs, meaningless threats and off-the-wall punishments, because they are emotional and often inappropriate, are an invitation to challenge and anger. Because they disregard a child's feelings, they send a message to the child that says, "I don't like you." Hostile responses tear down a child's self-esteem and are ultimately damaging. The words your child hears from you will become the way he feels about himself.

Learn to speak so your child will listen.

Don't beg. Don't get angry. Don't become exasperated. Instead, when making a request of your child, be calm and use direct statements that send your child this message: "This is what I expect you to do."

"Ryan, I want the garbage taken out now."

"Kara, I expect the laundry to be folded by dinnertime."

"Tina, I want you to clean your room before you go out and play."

Confident, clear and direct statements get results.

And if your child argues?

Above all, don't argue back. Do not get involved in a discussion. It will get you nowhere. The following scene illustrates this point:

Parent: *Ryan, the garbage is still in the kitchen and it's eight o'clock.*

Child: *Don't worry, I'll take it out. Just hang on until this show is over. It's my favorite.*

Parent: *It's always one more favorite show with you. And then I end up taking out the garbage.*

Child: *What are you talking about? I took it out the other night.*

Parent: *If I recall, I'm the one who had to take it out last night.*

Child: *Big deal. I do it most of the time.*

> **Parent:**   *If you did it most of the time we wouldn't be having this problem.*

What happened here? By arguing—by getting into a pointless discussion—the parent has lost control of the situation. Now she's even ended up in a position of defending herself! And the garbage is still sitting in the kitchen.

What should you do in a situation like this?

Don't argue. Use the "broken record" technique.

First, very clearly tell your child what you want him to do. If he argues, simply repeat the statement, as if you were a broken record. Do not argue back or even discuss the issue. Repeat your expectation.

For example:

> **Parent:**   *Ryan, I want you to take the garbage out now.*

> **Child:**   *Don't worry, I'll take it out. Just hang on until this show is over. It's my favorite.*

> **Parent:**   *I understand you want to finish the show, but I want you to take the garbage out now.*

> **Child:**   *That's not fair. I never get to see this show.*

> **Parent:**   *I understand you think it's not fair, but I want you to take the garbage out now.*

By staying firm, not arguing, not getting sidetracked, chances are good your child will comply with your request. You may hear grumbling and complaining, but your child will probably get up and take care of the job.

If necessary, back up your words with actions.

If, however, after three repetitions of your expectations your child still does not comply, it's time to back up your words with actions and present your child with a clear choice:

> **Parent:** *Ryan, I expect you to take the garbage out now. If you choose not to do your job you will choose to lose phone privileges tonight and tomorrow. The choice is yours.*

By giving your child a choice, you place responsibility for what happens right where it belongs—squarely on your child's shoulders.

Try these techniques the next time your child balks at fulfilling a responsibility or responding to a request. Just take a deep breath and follow through calmly and confidently. You'll find that this approach does work!

Parents Want to Know

Q & A

Household jobs are a part of every family's life. After all, these jobs are the day-to-day responsibilities that keep families organized, on track, and functioning smoothly.

Unfortunately, ongoing conflict over household jobs is a part of most families' lives, too. If you expect your child to help around the house you probably have encountered some problems of your own.

Let's look at some common questions parents ask about this subject—questions you may have wondered about also:

Question: *I am forever reminding my eleven-year-old daughter to do her chores. Not only does she procrastinate with her household jobs, but also with her homework, piano practice, and other responsibilities. What can I do?*

Answer: It sounds like your daughter needs some help managing her time. This can be easy and fun. Using the Job Squad Daily Planner on pages 62–63, have your daughter write in all her planned activities for a day plus free-time activities such as playing with friends, reading, or watching a favorite television show. By writing things down, she will see that everything can get done on time if it's planned. Most important, reward her when she is punctual with her household duties, practice and homework with kind words, a big hug and maybe a P.S. I Love You Coupon (pages 69–70). For more ideas for showing your appreciation, turn to pages 25–28.

Question: *I have two sons and a daughter. How can I be fair when handing out household jobs?*

Answer: Rotating job responsibilities is the most equitable way to make sure everyone is treated fairly. Refer to pages 15–18 for several ways to make dispensing of household duties more fun and fair.

Question: *My ten-year-old son refuses to clean up his room. Can you help?*

Answer: Cleaning up one's room is a reasonable responsibility for a ten-year-old child. But you have a responsibility, too. Have you taught your son how you expect him to clean his room? Do you help him plan when to do this job? And most important, do you praise him each time he follows through? If he still doesn't cooperate, though, a Job Squad Contract between the two of you can help. (Refer to pages 39–42.)

Question: *At what age should I have my child help with simple jobs around the house?*

Answer: Don't wait until your child is a teenager and expect a willing partner in household jobs. It won't happen! It's important to give children a sense of responsibility at an early age. Most children by the age of three can do a variety of helpful jobs around the house—picking up toys, removing their own plates from the table, getting a clean diaper for the baby, helping wash the car or water the plants.

Question: *How can I help my son keep on track with his daily jobs?*

Answer: Household jobs help a child learn responsibility and become self-reliant. But these goals won't be achieved if you let your child's participation slip or if you do the jobs for your child. Place a wipe-off chart on the refrigerator that lists your son's jobs. Each time he completes a job, place a check mark on the chart. At the end of a week or two, reward your child with a hug and a special P.S. I Love You Coupon. And don't forget to praise your child's accomplishments. (Refer to pages 25–28.)

Question: *Should I give my child an allowance for doing daily chores?*

Answer: Most experts say no. Household jobs are a responsibility that all family members should willingly share. In other words, children need to learn that some things we do simply because we are part of a family. When you pay someone for performing a task you are really giving a choice: "Do this and get paid. Don't do it and you won't get paid." Household jobs are not a choice. They are the responsibility of all family members. On the other hand, it is sometimes appropriate for children to be allowed to earn extra money by taking on extra chores if they've done their basic work around the house. This helps young children see the relationship between work and money without thinking that they should be paid for everything they do at home.

Question: *My child does such a sloppy job cleaning up the kitchen that I'd almost rather do it myself. What should I do?*

Answer: It's important to realize that it's not how a child completes a task, but the attitude and responsibility that is most important. The first thing you should ask yourself is, "Have I shown my child how to do the job?" Many household jobs require that children learn skills that they may not already possess. Break the job down in several easy steps. Then model each step. (Refer to pages 19–21.)

Question: *How can I let my child know how much I appreciate her help?*

Answer: Give yourself a pat on the back for asking! Nothing makes a child feel better than to receive praise and recognition from a parent. And your own words of praise carry the most meaning of all. Kind words and a big hug let your child know how much you appreciate her hard work and important contribution to the family. (Refer to pages 25–28.)

Top 10 Reminders

FOR ENDING THE CHORES WARS

You Job Squad Program is under way. Congratulations! With continued attention, most of your family chores wars can be a thing of the past. Here then are our top ten "chores wars" reminders to help you keep your new routine running smoothly. Refer to these reminders from time to time to give yourself a quick refresher when needed.

1. It's a great idea to start giving your children small responsibilities around the house while they are still very young. (Even three-year-olds can put toys away or help sort laundry.) Children are never too young to start feeling like a contributing part of the family. As they grow older, they'll understand that their contributions are both appreciated and needed—a real self-esteem booster.

2. No matter how old your children are, always teach them how a job should be done, step by step. Expect to repeat these "lessons" many times as your children learn new skills.

3. Praise your children whenever they help. Remember, your goal with children (especially younger ones) is not just to get extra household help, but to give them an opportunity to shine and feel the pride of accomplishment.

4. Don't get angry or frustrated when jobs aren't done to your satisfaction. Trial and error is an inevitable part of learning. It's more important that your children feel pride for having tried— and gain the confidence to try again.

5. Ask your children which jobs they would like to be responsible for. Budding interests can often be combined with household responsibilities. A child who loves the garden can be given jobs in the yard. A child who likes to cook can help you with dinner or help pack school lunches.

6. Rotate jobs among children so least desirable responsibilities can be fairly shared.

7. Children will complain about having to do household jobs. Stay firm! Doing chores is an important part of growing up and you have every right to expect your children to take part. Keep in mind that they are learning more than simply how to do a job. They are also learning to accept responsibility, see a job through and do their best work.

8. Remember—your children's allowance shouldn't be tied to household responsibilities. Your children should be expected to take part in chores because they are members of the family, not to get paid.

9. Make sure your children know exactly which jobs they are to do each day and each week. Children can't be expected to fulfill their responsibilities if those responsibilities aren't clearly spelled out. A quick "clean the bathroom after school" called out as you leave the house in the morning isn't enough. Your children need to have their regular jobs spelled out ahead of time. Once they know what you expect, written notes are a great way to give gentle reminders as time goes by.

10. Listen to your children. If there's a problem getting jobs done find out why and take steps to help them solve the problem.

Job Squad Worksheets

PLANNING SHEETS,
NOTES AND AWARDS

On the following pages are the worksheets that were introduced in this book. (You may want to enlarge them so that they are easier to fill in.) Make additional copies before using so there will always be an ample supply on hand.

Job Squad Planning Sheet

Help Wanted Ads

Spin-A-Job

Job Squad Daily Planner

Job Squad Tracker

Job Squad Contract

Job Swap Tickets

P.S. I Love You Coupons

Super Job Squad Award

Wonderful Week Job Squad Award

Job Squad
Planning Sheet

Household Job

Household Job

Household Iob

Household Job

Household Job

Household Job

Household Iob

Household Job

Household Job

Household Job

Household Job

Household Job

Write down all the household jobs that need to be done.
Write down the initials of family members who can do each job.

Job Squad
Planning Sheet

_____   _____
Household Job

_____   _____
Household Job

_____   _____
Household Job

_____   _____
Household Job

_____   _____
Household Job

_____   _____
Household Job

_____   _____
Household Job

_____   _____
Household Job

_____   _____
Household Job

_____   _____
Household Job

_____   _____
Household Job

_____   _____
Household Job

Write down all the household jobs that need to be done.
Write down the initials of family members who can do each job.

Job Squad Gazette

EXTRA!!! EXTRA!!! EXTRA!!!

Help Wanted!

Job Title: _____

Job Description: _____

_____

_____

_____

_____

Apply To: _____

Job Squad Gazette

EXTRA!!! EXTRA!!! EXTRA!!!

Help Wanted!

Job Title: _____

Job Description: _____

_____

_____

_____

_____

Apply To: _____

SPIN-A-JOB

Write a different household job in each part of the Spin-A-Job wheel.
Cut out both wheel and spinner. Attach spinner to wheel with a brad.
(For a more durable wheel, paste on cardboard before cutting.)

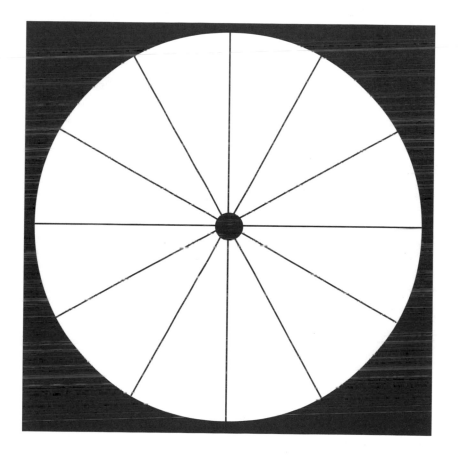

THIS JOB'S ● FOR YOU!

Job Squad
Daily Planner

For _____

Fill in your morning, afternoon and evening jobs
for each day of the week.

Sunday

Morning	Afternoon	Evening

Monday

Morning	Afternoon	Evening

Tuesday

Morning	Afternoon	Evening

Job Squad
Daily Planner

Wednesday

Morning	Afternoon	Evening

Thursday

Morning	Afternoon	Evening

Friday

Morning	Afternoon	Evening

Saturday

Morning	Afternoon	Evening

Good Job!

Job Squad Tracker

	S	M	T	W	T	F	S
	☐	☐	☐	☐	☐	☐	☐

Household Job

	S	M	T	W	T	F	S
	☐	☐	☐	☐	☐	☐	☐

Household Job

	S	M	T	W	T	F	S
	☐	☐	☐	☐	☐	☐	☐

Household Job

	S	M	T	W	T	F	S
	☐	☐	☐	☐	☐	☐	☐

Household Job

	S	M	T	W	T	F	S
	☐	☐	☐	☐	☐	☐	☐

Household Job

	S	M	T	W	T	F	S
	☐	☐	☐	☐	☐	☐	☐

Household Job

	S	M	T	W	T	F	S
	☐	☐	☐	☐	☐	☐	☐

Household Job

	S	M	T	W	T	F	S
	☐	☐	☐	☐	☐	☐	☐

Household Job

	S	M	T	W	T	F	S
	☐	☐	☐	☐	☐	☐	☐

Household Job

	S	M	T	W	T	F	S
	☐	☐	☐	☐	☐	☐	☐

Household Job

Each day you complete your job, check off the day of the week.
When each job has a full week of successful completion,
you will receive a special reward.

Good Job!

Job Squad Tracker

	S	M	T	W	T	F	S
	☐	☐	☐	☐	☐	☐	☐

Household Job

	S	M	T	W	T	F	S
	☐	☐	☐	☐	☐	☐	☐

Household Job

	S	M	T	W	T	F	S
	☐	☐	☐	☐	☐	☐	☐

Household Job

	S	M	T	W	T	F	S
	☐	☐	☐	☐	☐	☐	☐

Household Job

	S	M	T	W	T	F	S
	☐	☐	☐	☐	☐	☐	☐

Household Job

	S	M	T	W	T	F	S
	☐	☐	☐	☐	☐	☐	☐

Household Job

	S	M	T	W	T	F	S
	☐	☐	☐	☐	☐	☐	☐

Household Job

	S	M	T	W	T	F	S
	☐	☐	☐	☐	☐	☐	☐

Household Job

	S	M	T	W	T	F	S
	☐	☐	☐	☐	☐	☐	☐

Household Job

	S	M	T	W	T	F	S
	☐	☐	☐	☐	☐	☐	☐

Household Job

	S	M	T	W	T	F	S
	☐	☐	☐	☐	☐	☐	☐

Household Job

Each day you complete your job, check off the day of the week.
When each job has a full week of successful completion,
you will receive a special reward.

Job Squad Contract

The new rule in our house will be:

_____
New rule

If _____
Child's Name

does follow the rule,

_____
Reward

_____

If _____
Child's Name

does not follow the rule,

_____
Consequence

_____

_____
Parent's Signature

_____
Child's Signature

_____
Date

Job Squad

JOB SWAP TICKET

We have agreed to swap jobs for a day/week.

This is the job I will swap:

_____

Description of job

_____

Signature #1

This is the job I will swap:

_____

Description of job

_____

Signature #2

JOB SWAP TICKET

We have agreed to swap jobs for a day/week.

This is the job I will swap:

_____
Description of job

_____
Signature #1

This is the job I will swap:

_____
Description of job

_____
Signature #2

Super!

_____

♥ P.S. I Love You!

Thank You!

_____

♥ P.S. I Love You!

Good Work!

_____

♥ P.S. I Love You!

Use these coupons to write a caring note to your child or to present a special reward.

Super!

♥ P.S. I Love You!

Thank You!

♥ P.S. I Love You!

Good Work!

♥ P.S. I Love You!

Use these coupons to write a caring note to your child or to present a special reward.

SUPER

Job Squad

AWARD

Congratulations to

_____
Child's name

for keeping up the good work.

Let's celebrate by

_____

_____

_____

_____
Parent's Signature

_____
Date

WONDERFUL WEEK

Job Squad Award

is hereby awarded to

_____

Child's Name

FOR A WEEK'S WORTH
OF WONDERFUL WORK.

Thanks for doing such a great job!

_____

Parent Signature

_____

Date